Quilters
Questions

A Book of Curious Queries

By Kyra E. Hicks

What's your favorite
question?..

Enjoy,
Kyra E. Hicks
2014

Black Threads Press
Arlington, Virginia

ISBN: 0-9824796-4-6
Library of Congress Control Number: 2014950120

Library of Congress subject headings:
1. Conversation
2. Quilting – Miscellaneous
3. Quilting – United States
4. Humor & Entertainment – Puzzles & Games
   – Quizzes

Cover Design: Praveen007
Layout: Karen Krug
Edited by: Kira Freed, Sharon Honeycutt
Chief Motivator: Zoe Waller

Mississippi quilter Gwendolyn Magee
(1943–2011)

Your laughter and creativity are still missed.

Introduction

As a quilter, my shelves are filled with quilt magazines, how-to books, and quilt history tomes. I'm sure your shelves are similar. What we don't have is a book that helps us explore who we are as quiltmakers—something that helps us understand how we see ourselves, what we hold dear and infuse into our craft, how we want others to see us, and even what our legacy as quilters might be.

Quilters Questions features more than three hundred open-ended queries that probe feelings and opinions across a broad range of topics, including quilter identity, motivation, fabric obsession, sewing friends, quilt designs and more.

Quilters Questions can be read on your own or as a fun quilt guild activity. There are no right or wrong answers—just hours of fun and reflection.

What's your favorite question?

Enjoy!

Kyra E. Hicks
Arlington, VA
Black.Threads@yahoo.com

Quilters
Questions

1

Would you accept $25,000 to stop quilting forever? What if the offer were only $2,000?

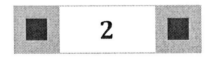

2

Describe your all-time favorite quilt.

3

If you could host a quilting party with three famous people - living or late - who would be included? Why?

4

Has the type of fabrics you purchase or use for your quiltmaking changed over time? If so, how?

5

You are visiting the local Goodwill store and see a pile of quilts. In the pile is a quilt you hand stitched for a neighbor as a gift. What do you do? Would you react differently if you had handmade the quilt for a family member or coworker?

6

There are glow-in-the-dark knitting needles, crochet hooks, and even thread. Do you think that glow-in-the-dark sewing needles or straight pins are something that might catch on?

7

In the U.S., National Quilting Day, the third Saturday in March, is set aside to celebrate the community of quilters and the tradition of quiltmaking. Do you usually participate in this annual celebration? If so, how?

8

Some musicians have created their most popular songs while under the influence of drugs and/or alcohol. Have you ever designed or stitched a quilt while under such influences? What did you think of the outcome?

9

What does it mean to be a quilter? Would you still call yourself a quilter if you hadn't made a quilt in more than ten years? Five years? Two years?

10

Have you ever participated in a yarn bombing? Why or why not? Would you ever participate in a quilt bombing?

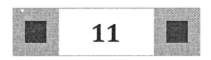

11

Would you rather have one of your quilts exhibited in an exclusive New York art gallery seen by 500 people or on a YouTube video seen by 5,000? Why?

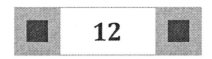

12

Your arthritis is getting to be a problem when cutting fabrics for your quilts. Do you think it is reasonable to ask your significant other to help you with this task? Why or why not?

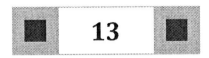

13

What do you give a quilter who has everything?

14

What types of events have you commemorated through your quilts? Why did you choose those events?

15

Do you think one of your quilts will survive for 100 years? If so, how would you describe the quilt? Why this one?

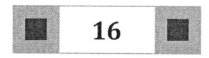

16

A friend is willing to pay you to use your longarm machine to bind and quilt a piece she's just completed. Her quilt has a sexual theme. Do you accept the work? Why or why not?

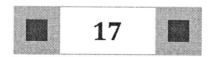

17

You attend an Independence Day celebration and see a family picnicking on a full-sized quilt featuring an American flag design. Do you think it is appropriate for them to sit, stand, or eat on the quilt given the design? Why or why not?

18

Is there a type of holiday fabric or design you'd like to find but haven't yet been able to? Have you ever written to your favorite fabric manufacturer to request the print? If so, what was the response?

19

You are asked to develop a quilt that features the images, themes or storylines from a major television program currently on the air. Which program would you choose? Why? Can you describe your quilt concept?

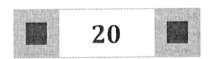

20

Do you have a room of your own for quilting? If so, how long have you had it? How did it come to be your quilting studio?

21

Your house is burning and you can only carry one quilt out quickly and safely. Do you grab a quilt you made or one made by someone else? Why is this quilt special to you?

22

Would you prefer to leave your quilts to your family, or a museum, or be sold at auction? Have you made formal arrangements for your quilts?

23

Would you consider any of your quilts to be examples of feminist art? If so, can you describe one such quilt?

24

Do you think that Hollywood and the entertainment industry are overlooking a major slice of society by not making any big-budget programs that are specifically about quilting or quilters?

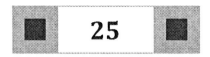

25

You sign up for a quilting class only to discover that most of the students are far more advanced in their skills than you. Do you think you will learn something from them, or do you drop out and take a different class?

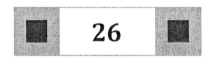

26

Children grow and mature into adults. In what ways has your quiltmaking evolved over the years?

27

Would you describe your sewing machine as an ex-husband, a faithful friend, or a seductive lover?

28

There is a large quilt show in your area each year, and your husband always attends with you. Do you reciprocate by attending a show or event that highlights one of his cherished hobbies? Do you encourage him equally?

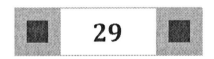

29

How does your quilting guild preserve its history? Has your guild ever considered sharing a printed copy of its history with the local historical society, the International Quilt Study Center Library, the Great Lakes Quilt Center at Michigan State University Museum, or another quilting research center? Why or why not?

30

You've been asked to participate in the making of a group quilt. Prior to joining, you learn that the theme of the quilt will be human sexuality. Would you still participate in the group quilting activity? Why or why not?

31

Do you incorporate your culture into your quiltmaking? If so, how?

32

Would you be offended if a couple implied to you that the lovely double wedding ring quilt you made for them was "put to good use" during their honeymoon? Why or why not?

33

Is the time you spend quilting each month equal to a part-time job, a full-time job, or a coffee break?

34

Have you incorporated any recycling, upcycling or "green" techniques into your quiltmaking? If so, what do you do?

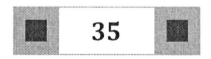

35

How long does it typically take you to stitch a quilt from concept to complete and bound quilt?

26

Do you own a quilt stitched by three or more generations in the same family? If so, do you use the quilt, display it, or keep it stored away? To whom do you want the quilt to go when you pass away? Why?

37

What are the three most important reasons you quilt?

38

Have you ever seen a garment on someone that you wanted to cut a piece of material from for a quilt you were working on? Have you ever done so?

39

Your best quilting friend has recently found a new quilting partner who has a lot more free time to spend doing projects together. Do you think that this will affect the quilting that you do on your own now?

40

Quilters can locate fabric for a quilt project practically anywhere. What is the most unusual place you've acquired fabrics?

41

Your friend's boyfriend seems to resent the one day each week when she attends the quilting group you belong to. Do you think this will negatively impact their relationship? Why or why not?

42

Have you ever read about artists who had non-supportive relatives or perhaps someone in their life who was jealous of their artistic success? How would you deal with such a situation?

43

Do you believe that enslaved Americans during the nineteenth century encoded secret messages or directions for escaping slavery into quilts? Why or why not?

44

Describe your dream quilting-related vacation.

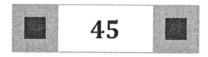

45

What is your favorite fabric selection or quilt-related smartphone app? What is the app called?

46

Alabama quiltmaker Nora Ezell (1917 – 2007), in her autobiography *My Quilts and Me: The Diary of an American Quilter*, shared that she set the price of one of her quilts by keeping a detailed record of the time spent making the quilt and the actual cost of the materials, including the fabric and thread. How do you determine the price to charge for one of your quilts?

47

Do you prefer to quilt by yourself or with a group? What environmental elements, such as music, room temperature, or refreshments, are important to you when quilting?

48

Have you been inspired by the Slow Stitching Movement introduced by internationally-known quilter Mark Lipinski? Slow Stitching involves slowing down to focus on "recharging" one's passion for fiber and needle arts while more deeply exploring one's creativity. Have you considered joining? Have you made a quilt or fiber art piece in the context of Slow Stitching?

49

Do you think that quilts entered into competitions should always be differentiated by those made entirely by hand and those made with sewing machines? Why or why not?

50

What are the top three reasons you attend quilting classes or workshops? At what point do you think you'll stop taking classes or workshops?

51

You are not close to your granddaughter, but you want to send her off to college with something handmade by you. You find out the colors of her school. Do you make her a stylish school-themed quilt or quilted wallhanging for her dorm? How do you think she'll react to your gift?

52

What are the top two ways you prefer to learn about new quilting techniques?

☐ Teach yourself

☐ Take a class or workshop

☐ View The Quilt Show episodes

☐ Watch a YouTube video

☐ Ask a friend to show you

☐ Something else? _____

53

More than three million viewers tune in to each episode of the BBC's *The Great British Sewing Bee*. Do you believe that there would be any interest in a reality show based on quilting in the U.S.? What type of quilt challenges would you like to see on such a program?

54

How, if at all, do you share what you've learned about quiltmaking with others?

55

How old is the oldest quilt you have that has never been washed?

56

Some old buildings are converted into artists' studios. Would you consider renting a small studio space if it meant being able to interact with other artists or quilters more often? Why or why not?

57

Sometimes art is closely tied to the artist's location, such as Southern writers, Hollywood actors, Broadway dancers or Gee's Bend quilters. To what degree do you consider your quiltmaking a reflection of your location?

58

Which television show would you like to see produced with a quilting theme? Would you watch any of the following programs?

☐ *America's Got Quilting Talent*

☐ *Antique Quilts Roadshow*

☐ *Law & Order: Paducah*

☐ *Mad Quilting Men*

☐ *Major Quilting Crimes*

☐ *Project Quilting*

☐ *Quilting with the Stars*

☐ *Quilt History Detectives*

☐ *Sew You Think You Can Dance*

59

What other hobbies or crafts would you devote time and energy to if you did not quilt?

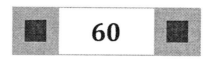

60

Over the years, you have acquired several quilts made by older family members who have passed away. The children and grandchildren of these family members are still living. Do you offer the quilts to any of the children or grandchildren of the now deceased quilters? Why or why not?

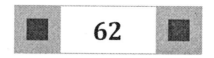

61

For which holidays do you purchase holiday-themed fabrics? Do you purchase such fabrics annually? Why or why not?

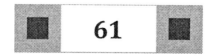

62

Do you keep a sketchbook or file with quilt ideas? What kind of details do you tend to capture in your quilting notes?

63

Do you think people will still use traditional bed quilts in fifty years or will quilts become more of an art form limited to display rather than actual use?

64

Do you consider your quiltmaking a feminist expression? Why or why not?

Below is a list of quilting-related mystery series. Have you read any of the novels in these whodunit series?

- ☐ A Benni Harper Mystery series by Earlene Fowler
- ☐ The Harriet Truman/Loose Threads mysteries by Arlene Sachitano
- ☐ A Quilters Club Mystery series by Marjory Sorrell Rockwell
- ☐ The Quilting Cozy Series by Carol Dean Jones
- ☐ The Quilting Mystery Series by Terrie Thayer
- ☐ Queen Bees Quilt Mysteries by Sally Goldenbaum and Marnette Farley
- ☐ A Shipshewana Amish Mystery series by Vannetta Chapman
- ☐ A Someday Quilt Mystery series by Clare O'Donahue
- ☐ Southern Quilting Mystery series by Elizabeth Craig

66

Do you ever visit eBay.com to view ephemera quilt materials? If so, how frequently? How would you describe the item you spent the most time locating?

67

How many quiltmaking classes and workshops do you attend per year? Do you foresee taking more or fewer classes next year?

68

You have a favorite quilt frame that is not in use, and a friend who has just taken up quilting asks to borrow it. Do you let him or her borrow it for what might be a long time or do you help your friend find one on sale?

69

Nancy Zieman has hosted the U.S. television program *Sewing with Nancy* for more than thirty years. Are you a fan of this public TV show? What makes this program a favorite? Have you ever made a donation to your local PBS station that carries this or other quilting programs?

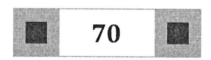

70

Do you hide your fabric purchases from your significant other?

71

UK fashion designer Jasper Conran created Look 47 (Spring/Summer 2013), a striking, contemporary maxi dress based on a Grandmother's Flower Garden pattern. Have you ever made a garment based on a traditional quilt pattern? Why or why not? If so, what was the garment and what pattern did you use?

72

What three people have had the greatest influence on your quiltmaking? Why are they so influential?

73

Today's quilters have longarm machines, basting guns, and other modern tools to make quilting easier. Do you think the more traditional techniques will eventually die out? If so, which techniques do you see going away?

74

Do you sing while quilting? If so, do you sing to recorded music or *a capella*?

75

Do you need one or two hands to count on your fingers the number of sewing machines you own?

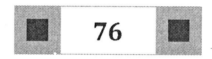

76

You make a quilt with a bold color scheme and your fellow quilters seem to have negative opinions about it. Do you heed their criticism, or do you go ahead and display your inventive work?

77

What is your favorite children's picture book with a quilting theme?

78

You are attending a local rummage sale at a synagogue in town and see that the small quilt you made for a charity auction is among the discarded linens. What do you do?

79

Do you have a quilt scrapbook or other documentation of your quilts? Is it for your eyes only or do you let others look at it?

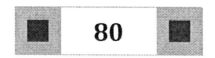

80

Many of us get an annual medical check-up or work-related performance review. Once a year, do you formally spend time alone reflecting on your quilting accomplishments? Why or why not?

81

Your quilts are part of a local exhibition. What would you like exhibit visitors to remember about you or your quilts?

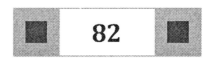

82

Are you familiar with any of the English and Spanish bilingual children's picture books and quilt patterns by Jane Tenorio-Coscarelli?

☐ *The Burrito Boy*

☐ *The Piñata Quilt*

☐ *The Tamale Quilt*

☐ *The Tortilla Quilt Story*

83

The maintenance man at your church always makes sure that the community room is in perfect order for your quilting group. Do you think it is a good idea to make him a quilt in honor of his support?

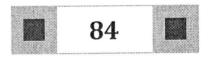

84

Would you purchase a mystery box of quilting ephemera for $25 or less? What if the box cost $100? What treasures would you hope the box contained?

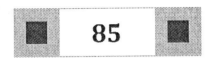

85

What do you uniquely bring to quilting?

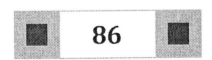

86

Do you make quilts primarily for utility or for art? Why?

87

You are part of a quilting group and a member asks for your help on a quilt at her home. You give her several hours of your time. She later wins a prize for the quilt but doesn't mention your assistance. How do you feel? Do you let anyone know you helped her with the prize-winning quilt?

88

Different factors make a successful quilter. What percentage of the following factors makes you a successful quilter?

Time	_____%
Talent	_____%
Money	_____%
Support from Others	_____%
Internal Drive	_____%
Total	100%

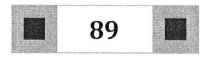

89

Do you think someone decades from now might confirm the authenticity of one of your quilts by your DNA or fingerprints *inside* the quilt layers?

90

How many quilts do you make in a typical year? Do you anticipate making more or fewer quilts this year? Why?

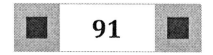

91

The coffee house has monthly art displays by local painters. Would you consider proposing to the manager that she exhibit your quilts one month? Why or why not?

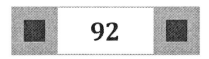

92

Have you ever made a quilt based on a science fiction program such as *Star Trek, Star Wars,* or *Doctor Who?* If so, can you describe your quilt and share what inspired you to create the design?

93

How important has rejection been to your growth as a quilter?

94

What new technique do you wish to learn and incorporate into your quiltmaking? Why?

95

What is your response to the *Quilting in America™ 2010* survey, which revealed that most dedicated quilters own 2.7 sewing machines, and 25% of all quilters own at least 4 sewing machines? How many is too many sewing machines for one quilter?

96

Do you have a last will and testament? Have you left instructions about your favorite quilts? Your fabric stash? Your quilt-related library? Your sewing machines? Your good scissors?

97

Does a smoke-scented quilt bother you?

98

Imagine a religious leader you admire is also a quilter. Who is this leader, and what kind of quilts would he or she stitch?

99

You hear about a quilting group that meets twice a month at a local restaurant. Would you attend sessions to work on your quilting project, or do you think it would be too distracting?

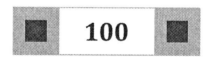

100

Who or what initially motivated you to learn how to make quilts? Was your physical location important to your decision to start quilting?

101

Have the quilts you made in your 20s, 30s, or 40s varied from the quilts you made in your 50s, 60s, or 70s? How?

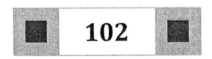

102

Have you ever participated in the making of a group quilt? What were the most and least enjoyable aspects of the group experience?

103

Do you believe your level of enthusiasm for a project would be different if you were doing it on your own compared to working with a group of fellow quilters? Why or why not?

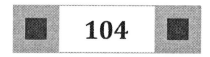

104

Artists such as painter and photographer David Hockney create original artwork using an Apple iPad. Have you ever designed a quilt pattern on an iPad? If so, what made the experience unique for you?

105

Have you ever had a disagreement with anyone over quilting? Describe what sparked the difference and how it was resolved.

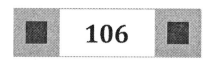

106

Who, living or late, do you wish could view your quilts? Why?

107

If you had to suffer one illness or affliction that could affect your quiltmaking, which would you choose: rheumatoid arthritis in your hands, cataracts, color blindness, or severely burned fingers? Why would you choose that particular affliction? As a quilter, which condition would you absolutely not want to have?

108

If you receive an invitation or catalog from a quilt show, do you keep it as a source of inspiration or even copy some of the quilts or ideas you find in it?

109

How, if at all, do your political beliefs influence your quiltmaking?

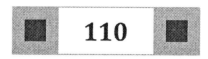

110

Are you a first-generation quilter? How important is it to pass along your quiltmaking skills to the next generation in your family?

111

Are there artistic concerns, themes or subject matters you consistently explore in your quilts? Can you name two?

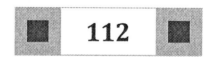

112

Since 2003, the Quilts of Valor, a grassroots effort, has provided returning war veterans with a quilt in appreciation for their wartime service. More than 95,000 lap-sized quilts have been stitched through January 2014. Has the Quilts of Valor project come to your community yet? Would you be open to participating in it?

113

Do you consider your quilts to
beautiful designs, functional covers, or pages
from your diary? Why?

114

Have you ever purchased fabric just because it
was appealing to you even though you had no
specific project in mind?

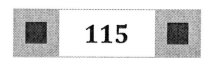

115

Have you ever had one of your quilts
professionally appraised? Were you surprised
to learn that your quilt was worth more or
less than you thought? Was your significant
other surprised by the valuation?

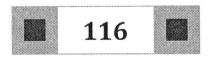

116

Your granddaughter loves to help with craft and quilt projects. At the end of the school year, she asks you to help her make a quilted wallhanging as a gift for her teacher. Do you think this is too much work for a teacher's gift? Why or why not?

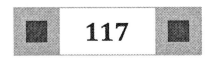

117

Many quilters use elaborate surface designs in their quilts. What is the "next new thing" you see in quiltmaking?

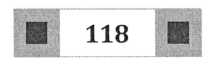

118

You are part of a quilting group, but you don't have the time or the budget of the others in the group. How does this make you feel?

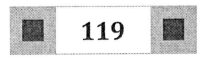

119

Do you think documents such as old quilting books and magazines, Mountain Mist® batting wrappers, and quilt guild newsletters have archival value and should be preserved? Why or why not?

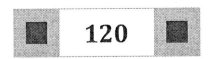

120

Have you ever made a quilt using alternatives to fabrics (e.g., wood, plastic, or paperclips)? Describe the alternative materials you used.

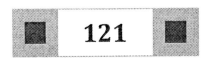

121

Have you ever made a quilt that has sexual overtones? If yes, have you ever publicly displayed the quilt?

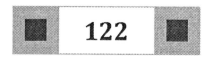

122

What are the most dangerous aspects of quilting for you?

123

When making a quilt from a pattern, how likely are you to follow the fabric recommendations exactly? How might you deviate from the recommendation?

124

How important is Internet access to your success as a quilter?

125

Your daughter is about to move in with her boyfriend. Though you worry about this sort of situation, you want them to know you wish them well. Is a handmade quilt too old-fashioned or too suggestive as a gift?

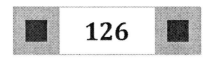

126

How do you determine the pattern or subject matter of your quilts?

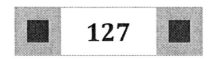

127

Do you watch any quilting-oriented shows on your public television or cable stations? If so, which are your favorite programs?

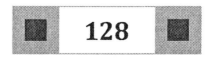

128

You made a fantastic quilt for your daughter's boyfriend only to find out after the two had split-up that he was a chronic cheater. Is it acceptable to ask for the quilt back? Why or why not?

129

What would motivate you to stitch a quilt and send it to your favorite celebrity? Who would that celebrity be?

130

Quilts are tangible and tactile. How much would you pay for magical fabric to make a liquid or an invisible quilt?

131

Have you been inspired by any of the following modern quilters?

☐ Alissa Haight Carlton

☐ Rashida Coleman Hale

☐ Elizabeth Hartman

☐ Yoshiko Jinzenji

☐ Rachel May

☐ Quilters of Gee's Bend

☐ Weeks Ringle

☐ Latifah Saafir

☐ Denyse Schmidt

☐ Angela Walters

If so, what aspect of their work stirs you?

132

What would you put into a time capsule to reflect or commemorate your quiltmaking?

133

A quilting competition is held by a regional arts group, and the winners will have their work displayed only through an online exhibition. Would you enter such a competition? Why or why not?

134

The International Federation for Robotics reported that in 2012, about 3 million robots were purchased for personal and domestic use. The robots performed tasks such as vacuum and floor cleaning, lawn mowing, and entertainment. Do you think robots will one day stitch a quilt based on your personal preferences? Why or why not?

135

Websites, such as Etsy.com, offer crafters and quilters an opportunity to sell their wares. Have you sold your quilts on such websites? Why or why not?

136

A friend who smokes gives you a beautiful handmade quilt she made that reeks of smoke. What, if anything, do you do to the quilt? Would your actions differ if the quilt was stitched by a coworker with little opportunity to see the quilt in your home?

137

In case of an emergency, does your significant other or family have access to a list of your quilts?

138

Have you ever paid as much for a sewing machine as you might pay for a good used car?

139

Have you ever loved a commissioned quilt you stitched so much that you ended up keeping the quilt or making a duplicate for yourself?

140

Your teenage granddaughter finally wants to learn to quilt and asks for your assistance. She has selected a sexual theme as her first quilt project. Do you give her all the help she needs to make the quilt, or do you try to convince her to select a different quilt theme? Why?

141

Have you ever sewn a note inside one of your quilts in hopes that it might be discovered years later? Why or why not?

142

If you could take a quilting cruise that combined quilting activities with travel to places such as the Caribbean, Alaska or the Mediterranean, would you want to go? Why or why not?

143

A couple has a wedding registry that includes a wedding ring quilt from a very pricey store. Do you think it would be acceptable to instead make a close copy out of materials you have at home? Why or why not?

144

A friend says that she has been using online videos from the YouTube website to learn about various quilting techniques. Have you ever considered making a YouTube video about some aspect of your quiltmaking? Why or why not?

145

What type of quilter do you consider yourself to be: beginner, intermediate, or advanced?

146

The U.S. Labor Department reported that the average American household spent just over $500 on their pets in 2011. Have you ever stitched a quilt especially for your own pet or someone else's?

147

Do you photograph each of your completed quilts? Why or why not?

148

Do you consider yourself to be a successful quilter? How do you define quilting success?

149

The Quilters Hall of Fame has honored individuals who have made outstanding contributions to quilting since 1980. Who would you nominate for next year's award and why?

150

Have you ever regretted giving someone a quilt you made? If so, why?

151

Some quilters keep a list of movies, television shows or plays in which quilts are part of the scene or set. Can you name such a performance? For bonus points, can you name the pattern of the quilt?

152

Over the course of your quilting career, how many quilts have you made?

153

Do you listen to music while quilting? Does the type of music you select vary depending on the quilt pattern you're making, or does it depend more on how you feel when you're quilting?

154

How welcomed would a member of the opposite sex be to your quilting guild?

155

Do you consider your quilting studio a functional space or a sacred space? Why?

156

Someone copies your quiltmaking style. How does this make you feel?

157

Do you have a quiltmaking or art-related resume? When was the last time you updated it?

158

Can you just look at a quilt and know that an African American or Amish quilter stitched it? How?

159

The popular television program *Project Runway* awarded its first season's prize to Jay McCarroll, a designer who incorporated quilting or patchwork into some of his creations. What do you think this means for fashion's view of quilting?

160

If you could pass on quilting as a family tradition, who in your family would you select to carry on the tradition? Why would you choose this person?

161

A coworker is planning a baby shower, and the baby's gender is unknown. You want to make a gender-neutral quilt. What colors of fabrics do you use?

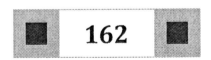

162

What are your three favorite quilting websites or blogs? What makes them your favorites?

163

A young person in your community is badly injured while serving in the armed forces. Would you be willing to take on the challenge of arranging for a community quilt to be made for that veteran during his or her time in the hospital? Why or why not?

164

If you didn't have your group of quilting friends to work with, do you think that you would be able to complete as many projects as you do right now? Why or why not?

165

You are looking at quilts on eBay.com and come across a quilt you stitched for a friend as a gift. What do you do? How would you feel if the quilt had been commissioned?

166

We expect to find quilt patterns in a quilt magazine. Which of today's magazines do you wish carried a quilt pattern that reflects the magazine's philosophy and target audience?

- ☐ *AARP*
- ☐ *Cosmopolitan*
- ☐ *Ebony*
- ☐ *Good Housekeeping*
- ☐ *Guideposts*
- ☐ *Reader's Digest*
- ☐ *National Geographic*
- ☐ *O, The Oprah Magazine*
- ☐ *People*
- ☐ *Sports Illustrated*

167

Has anyone ever asked you about the "blankets" you make? Do you find the word "blanket" verses "quilt" to be derogatory? Why or why not?

168

Do you have a unique technique or way of creating quilts that you want to share with others? If so, how do you act on this desire?

169

Have you ever added wearable technology or sound effects to one of your quilt creations? If so, what did you add and why?

170

In a pinch, you can use the middle segment of your index finger to measure an inch. What other unusual "tools" do you use in your quiltmaking?

171

Your friend complains about her husband frequently, but this is a man who has built her a sturdy quilting frame, converted the spare room to a sewing sanctuary, and supported her creative efforts. Do you point these things out to her? Why or why not?

172

Is there a quilter whose style of quiltmaking you'd like to replicate? What is it about his or her style that has made such an impression on you?

173

How many hours would you be willing to spend on making a quilt as a gift for a friend? Would the amount of time invested be more or less for a quilt made for a family member or charity project? Why?

174

Have you regularly downloaded quilting-related audio or video podcasts such as the American Patchwork & Quilting Podcast, Sandra Hasenauer's *Quilting ... For the Rest of Us*, *The Pioneer Quilter*, or *The History Quilter* podcasts? What quilting podcast would you recommend?

175

Your husband has just cleared out his closet and has asked you to take some jackets, ties, and T-shirts to the local charity shop. Do you think it is a better idea to make him a quilt from his old garments? Why or why not?

176

Basting is something that some quilters hate to tackle. While you are scouring the aisles or the website of your favorite quilt shop, you see a basting gun. Do you give it a try or stick with hand basting?

177

You have just completed a quilt that you feel is a true masterpiece. You decide to enter it in a national competition, but you see that there is a high entry fee. What is the highest fee you'd pay to potentially get your quilt in front of a large audience?

178

In a typical quilting guild meeting, do you listen, take notes, or talk more?

179

What is the value of your quilt collection? Have you had any of your quilts professionally appraised? Why or why not?

180

A round robin quilt project involves starting a quilt top and passing it along to others to add to, based on specific instructions, until the finished top comes back to you. In the meantime, you also add to the quilt tops of others in the round robin circle. Have you ever participated in a round robin project? Why or why not? Are round robins too old-fashioned for today's quilters?

181

What, if any, challenges do you feel a male quilter may have?

182

Do you have a formal inventory of the quilts you have made? How have you made your inventory (e.g., computerized, photographs, video, or a simple handwritten list)? How do you describe the quilts in your inventory records?

183

Is the monetary value of your fabric stash greater or less than the amount currently in your savings account?

184

How many months would you have to date someone before you made him or her a quilted wallhanging or full-sized quilt?

185

If there could magically be one more hour in each day, how many minutes would you devote to increased quilting activities?

186

Does your significant other and/or family respect your quilting room? In what ways?

187

Kickstarter, an online crowdsourcing service, is a way to potentially fund creative projects. Some have successfully funded quilting-related projects such as:

☐ Nadine Licostie, who raised $36,082 in 2014 to fund production for the film "*The Last One: Unfolding the AIDS Memorial Quilt*"

☐ Emily Fischer, who raised $149,301 in 2013 to fund the making of a Constellation Quilt to illustrate various celestial constellations

☐ Shelly Zegart, who raised $6,831 in 2012 to create "Why Quilts Matter" Conversation Guides

☐ Eliza Fernand, who raised $4,263 in 2011 to fund two Quilt Stories tours

Would you consider funding a dream quilting project through Kickstarter? Why or why not? Describe your proposed project.

188

What would motivate you to drive 40 miles or more each way to a fabric shop?

189

Do you think a quilter's sexual orientation influences his or her preferred quilting themes? Why or why not?

190

Can you just look at a quilt and know that a male quilter stitched it? If so, what gives it away?

191

Some singers are also quilters. Are you familiar with the songs of Cathy Miller, Canada's Singing Quilter? Her repertoire includes "100 Ways to Hide Your Stash", "A Quilt for Gran", "12 Step Plan for Quilters" and "I Remember You," written for Ami Sims' Alzheimer's Art Quilt Initiative.

192

Would you participate in a group quilting project that uses a theme meant to educate people about a cause? Why or why not? What would the cause be?

193

How much do you spend on fabric purchases in a given year? Is this more or less than your annual expenditure on clothing? Is it more or less than your retirement savings?

194

Have you considered learning new aspects of quilting through online or distance learning? Why or why not? Have you considered quilting programs from:

☐ The Academy of Quilting

☐ The American Quilter's Society (AQS) and West Kentucky Community & Technical College

☐ Craftsy.com

☐ TheQuiltShow.com

☐ The University of Nebraska – Lincoln Department of Textiles and Fashion Design (hybrid distance master's program)

195

Would you rather be a technically brilliant but slow-to-finish quilter, creatively inspired but average-in-skill quilter, or a prolific but moderately good quilter? Why?

196

Have you ever participated in a quiltmaking round robin? Have you ever stopped the round robin because you did not complete your assigned task?

197

How frequently do you use photo transfers in your quilting? What is your favorite photo transfer technique (e.g., iron-on transfer, Liquitex gel medium, or printing computer image on fabric)?

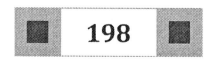

198

If you needed money, would you sell a quilt given to you as a gift? Why or why not?

199

Should quiltmaking be formally taught in public schools? Why or why not? If so, in what grade should the craft be introduced?

200

To what lengths would you go to track down an image of an amazing quilt displayed in an exhibit ten years ago? Name three sources you would use to track down the quilt image.

201

Several fiber art pieces were featured in the shocking 1976 book *Hardcore Crafts*, edited by Nancy Bruning Levine. This catalog featured crafts that reflected "our society's sexual freedom." If there was a call for submissions in an updated version of the book, would you submit a quilt or other fiber art piece? Why or why not?

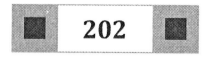

202

The average quilter has a whopping $8,000 in quilting tools and supplies, according to the *Quilting in America™ 2010* survey. If you had to cut back on quilting supply expenses, what would be the first thing you would stop buying? Why?

203

Portland textile artist Adriene Cruz sometimes heightens the viewer's experience of her quilts by sewing spices and other aromatic natural substances into her pieces. Have you ever deliberately added a fragrant substance to one of your quilts? Why or why not? If so, what substance did you add?

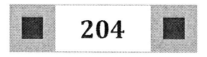

204

Some quilters also engage in other needlearts. Which of the following do you participate in?

☐ Beading

☐ Crochet

☐ Cross-Stitch

☐ Dollmaking

☐ Embroidery

☐ Knitting

☐ Sewing

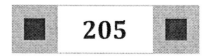

205

Have you ever been given a quilt as a gift and not liked the design? How did you respond?

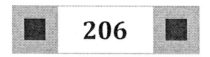

206

Quilting ephemera includes paper items that are meant for short-term use, such as postcards, exhibit programs, and magazine articles. Do you collect any quilting ephemera? If so, how would you describe your collection?

207

Have you ever designed your own fabric using an online service, such as Spoonflower.com, that prints custom fabrics? What was the primary reason you chose to design your own fabric? How did it feel when you first held your personally designed cloth?

208

Quilt historians use a variety of printed records such as census data, newspaper articles, diaries, church records, and family histories, to piece together a quilter's life. One hundred years from now, how will quilt historians learn about you and your quiltmaking?

209

Have you ever purchased a quilt or quilt-related item on eBay.com? What has been your most treasured find?

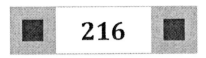

216

A time capsule is being prepared to send into outer space, and NASA is looking for a quilt to place in the capsule. What quilt or quilt pattern would you submit and why?

217

To the world, a UFO is a science fiction phenomenon. To a quilter, a UFO (unfinished object) is simply an adventure waiting to be completed. How many unfinished quilt projects do you have? How many of these do you admit to publicly? Are the two numbers different? Why?

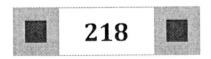

218

Is it important to you to have a quilt you made survive for 100 years? If so, what actions are you taking to ensure one of your quilts survives that long?

219

During Barack Obama's first presidential campaign, hundreds of quilters and crafters were inspired to stitched quilts and other art pieces about the historical political event. What might inspire you to create a quilt in support of a political candidate?

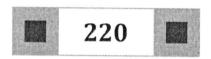

220

Have you ever stitched a quilt inspired by your nation's flag? If so, describe the quilt.

221

Do you think it would be unwise to choose a quilt with a sensual theme as a project for a group that consists of both men and women? Why or why not?

222

What underlies your commitment to quilting?

223

Not every quilt is a museum-quality work of art. Have you ever falsely complimented another quilter's work in progress or finished quilt? Why or why not?

224

Quilting is often associated with good fun. Are you familiar with the following women who promote quilting through humor? Who else would you add to the list?

☐ Lisa Boyer, author of *Stash Envy: And Other Quilting Confessions and Adventures*

☐ Katsy Chappell, the Quilting Comic

☐ Megan Dougherty, author of *Quilting Isn't Funny*

☐ Julia Icenogle, illustrator of the Mrs. Bobbins comic strip

225

Is guild membership important to your quiltmaking? Why or why not?

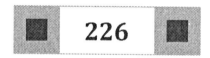

226

Can you name a favorite celebrity who quilts?

227

On a recent fabric-purchasing venture with a few quilting friends, you notice that one of them fails to buy anything (and this is the third time this has happened). Do you ask her if things are okay, stop inviting her, or ignore the friend's non-purchasing behavior? Why?

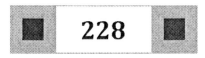

228

If one of your wildest quilting dreams were to come true, what would it be?

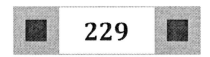

229

Your office does a "Secret Santa" every year and you decide that this would be a good time to make a small quilt. After the party, you overhear the colleague who received the quilt complaining that he or she didn't get a store-bought gift. How do you react?

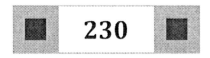

230

Do you think you have an identifiable quiltmaking style? How would you describe your style?

231

Do you think that a quilt based on the iconic television program *The Simpsons* would be as valuable and "artistic" as one based on a family-themed painting by Norman Rockwell?

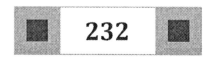

232

In 1991, Gloria Molina became the first Latina ever elected to the Los Angeles County Board of Supervisors. Supervisor Molina is a quilter and one of 70 members of The East Los Angeles Stitchers, also known as TELAS de la Vida. Is there an elected official in your community who also quilts or is a member of your local guild?

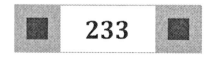

233

Do you feel comfortable going to a quilt exhibit by yourself? Why or why not?

234

You and someone in your quilting guild have similar fabric tastes. You see a fabric print that you just love, and you know that person in your guild would love it, too. There is only one yard left. What do you do?

235

If you were to become incapacitated, does your family know if you have any quilts out on loan, when those quilts should be returned, or who to contact to retrieve them?

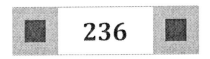

236

Pinterest is an online tool for "pinning" visual ideas on virtual bulletin boards. There are hundreds of boards on topics related to quilts, quilters, fabrics, how-to books, videos and more. Do you have a Pinterest account? What are your favorite quilting boards?

237

Since 1978, Eleanor Burns has thrilled and educated quilters through her accessible quiltmaking instructions. Are you most familiar with her *Quilt in a Day* projects from her pattern books, the PBS episodes, or quiltinaday.tv?

238

Do you call yourself a quilter if you only stitch your quilt tops and bottoms, but pay someone else to quilt and bind the pieces? Why or why not?

239

Just by looking at one of your quilts, do you think others can correctly identify your ethnicity? How about your religion? If so, what elements of your quiltmaking do you think provide the clues? Did you provide those clues intentionally?

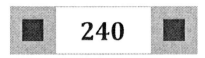

240

How did you learn to quilt? Who has been your most influential quilting teacher?

241

Is your family supportive of your quiltmaking? Is their support important to you? Why or why not?

242

A friend who is about to begin her first quilt asks you about essential quilting tools. Knowing that her budget is very limited, how would you advise her?

243

How large do you want the audience for your quilts to be? Is your target audience just yourself, your family, your personal friends, your local community, your regional community, your country, or the entire world?

244

Have you ever stitched a quilt that had sexual overtones? If yes, what prompted you to create the quilt?

245

Have you researched self-publishing a catalog of your quilts through services such as Blurb.com or CreateSpace.com? If not, do you have an interest in doing so?

246

Do you think the amount of color, sound, natural light, or inspirational images in your quilting studio or work space has a significant effect on the results of your quilting efforts? Why or why not?

247

What aspects, if any, of your personal quilting history are important to you? How are you actively preserving your history?

248

If the average age of today's quilter is sixty-two, does it mean that quilting is facing extinction? Do you think that society would really allow the art of quilting to come to an end? Why or why not?

249

Do you think of your quiltmaking as a contribution to your national quilt history or simply as a personal endeavor?

250

Are you addicted to fabric? How do you know?

251

If world leaders had to sit down at a quilting bee and participate in the creation of a quilt, do you think the act of quilting would produce a cooperative and healing atmosphere? Why or why not? Which world leaders would you require attend?

252

Would you invest in a "design wall" if you felt that it could really help you create the most imaginative quilts possible?

253

Have you ever donated a quilt for a charity fundraiser? Afterward, would you have preferred to have given money instead of the quilt?

254

A friend suggests that you develop a quilt that uses a social networking site as a theme. What site would you select? How would you go about designing this sort of quilt?

255

You see a quilt you stitched as a commissioned piece on exhibit under another quilter's name. What do you do?

256

Would you consider attending a quilting class in a museum or gallery where you could work surrounded by antique or high-art quilts? Why or why not?

257

Have you ever displayed one of your quilts with sexual overtones in public? Did you feel differently about exhibiting that quilt than a quilt with a more traditional theme?

258

If you could only purchase one yard of fabric, would it feature small florals, a holiday print, or an ethnic-inspired pattern?

259

If you wash your quilts, what is the longest span of time you have gone without washing one of the quilts?

260

You volunteer at a women's center that has decided to work on a "survivors' quilt" project that is meant to serve as a form of therapy for rape victims. These quilts are going to show the triumphs of overcoming challenges, but you are concerned about the conversation during quilting times. Would you participate?

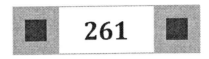

261

Do you typically machine wash or dry-clean your quilts?

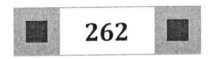

262

How familiar are you with quilting history in the context of lesbian art?

263

A friend who is an animal activist and serious vegetarian has just taken up quilting. While a lot of your quilting friends have been showering her with interesting gifts and tools, you want to give her a leather thimble because of its amazing usefulness. Do you think this is a good idea for a gift?

264

If you went to school for each year you have quilted, would you now be in elementary, middle school, high school, college, a graduate program, or working on your Ph.D?

265

You see that a family member is using a quilt you made as a tablecloth instead of a bedspread. The quilt is now stained and dirty. Do you ask the relative about his or her choice in using the quilt as a table covering? Why or why not?

266

Do you share your quiltmaking activities on social media websites or in online discussion groups? Do you ever print your comments to save for historical reasons? Do you believe your posts will help preserve your quilting legacy?

267

Are you a member of a quilting guild? How many quilting guilds do you belong to?

268

A friend makes a quilt for you, but it is really not your taste or style. Do you regift it to someone else, or do you put the handmade gift in a closet and use it when the friend visits?

269

Do you think there is quilting in heaven? If so, who would be at your quilting bee and why?

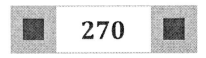

270

Do you keep a scrapbook with fabric swatches from the quilts or other textile projects you've worked on or completed? Why or why not?

271

Have you ever lost one of your quilts in the mail or had a quilt stolen? Did you consider using a service such as LostQuilt.com to try to recover the quilt? Why or why not?

272

If you did not have Internet access for 30 days - either through your computer or smartphone - would your quiltmaking be affected? If so, in what ways?

273

Your daughter brings her teenage son's old T-shirts – many of which contain objectionable images and words - to your house to have you make a quilt from them. You don't like the messages on the T-shirts. Do you agree to make the quilt? Why or why not?

274

If you only had a week to live, would you spend any time quilting? If so, would you make a quilt for yourself or someone else? Why? What else would you want to accomplish quilt-wise in that week? Why would that be your goal?

275

Do you prewash your fabrics before using the pieces in a quilt? Why or why not?

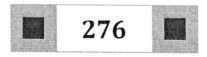

276

The Chattahoochee (GA) Evening Stars Quilt Guild, the Denton (TX) Quilt Guild and the Greater Ann Arbor (MI) Quilt Guild teach quilt-appreciation through a Storybook Quilts program. In this program children are read a quilt-themed picture book and shown an actual quilt based on the book. Have you ever made a storybook quilt? Why or why not? What favorite story have you or would you depict?

277

Can you name three male quilters?

278

Have you ever purchased an erotically-themed quilt? If so, where is it at this moment?

279

Would you still quilt if you could not use fabric to make the quilt? What alternative materials would you use?

280

On a cross-country flight, what quilt magazines, if any, do you take to read?

281

Would you still make quilts even if no one but you saw the finished pieces? Why or why not?

282

Since 2003, the Quilt Index (quiltindex.org) has documented quilt images, stories and quilter bios and made them available for the public's pleasure and education. Through the service, quilt collections from nearly forty sources as varied as state quilt documentation projects, the Daughters of the American Revolution (DAR) Museum, and the South Africa Quilt History Project, have been cataloged. Have you visited the Quilt Index online or downloaded its smartphone app? Do you have a quilt listed in the index?

283

Is religious faith important to your quilting? How, if at all, does your faith influence your quiltmaking?

284

Have you ever stitched a block for the AIDS Memorial Quilt Project? If so, who did you honor?

285

Are you familiar with the quilting-theme sci-fi novels *Death by Chenille*, or the sequel *When Chenille Is Not Enough* by Ann Anastasio and Lani Longshore?

286

Can you just look at a quilt and know that an Australian, Canadian, British or Japanese quilter stitched it? How?

287

Would you prefer to be an expert quilter known only to your local community or a mediocre quilter known nationally? Why?

288

If you were given fabric that had a very clear sensual motif, would you use it to make a quilt or tuck the material away for another day?

289

What would you do if you found out that your kids or grandkids had been using your fabric scissors for paper crafts and projects? Would you mind, purchase new ones, or get the old ones sharpened?

290

What are your best qualities that your quiltmaking highlights? What are your worst ones?

291

A member of your quilting guild seems to make the most beautiful things without any effort. Are you jealous of her skills and abilities, or are you just happy to see all the beautiful things she makes?

292

Consider the collection of quilts that you've made. If you make a new quilt, do you think others will know you were the quiltmaker just by looking at this new quilt? Is so, what characteristics would give it away as yours?

293

Have you been motivated by the modern quilt movement? Modern quilts are usually functional and are inspired by modern design aesthetics. What characteristics of modern quilting do you incorporate into your creations?

294

Do you think that social networking sites like Facebook, Twitter, Pinterest and Instagram are useful to a quilter? If so, how do you use them for your quiltmaking?

295

Is there a well-known quilter you admire the most? Why? Would it be important to you to share your admiration with the quilter? Why or why not?

296

Who is the primary audience for your quilts?

297

You make a family album quilt for your in-laws and receive a very appreciative thank-you note from them. The quilt, however, remains hidden away. Do you ask them about the quilt, or do you "let sleeping dogs lie"? Why?

298

Do you keep photos of, or magazine articles about, quilts made by others? How do these images influence your own quiltmaking?

299

Have you ever donated quilting fabrics or books to a prison quilting program?

300

Since 2002, the Coffee Creek Quilters have taught quilting classes to incarcerated women at a correctional facility in Wilsonville, Oregon. They even offer a 14-page guide from their website on how to start such a program. Have you ever volunteered to teach quilting at a local prison or correctional facility?

301

From pattern and fabric selection to finished quilt, describe your typical process for making a quilt.

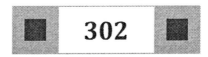

302

Do you want your obituary printed in the local newspaper? Would you want it to recall that you were a quilter? If so, are there other aspects of your quiltmaking life that you'd want published? If so, which ones?

303

Do you make a point of reading the blogs of other quilters and fabric artists in order to find out about events, trends, and new ideas? What are your three favorite quilting blogs?

304

Imagine that you complete a quilting project in a spare room that makes you feel a bit cramped, but you get the most praise you have ever received for that quilt. Would you continue to work in that space because of these results?

305

Do you find quilting addictive?

306

Would you ever make a quilt and send it to the president of the United States, the governor of your state, or the mayor of your city? If so, what would motivate you to make such a quilt?

307

Do you know American Sign Language (ASL)? Have you seen the amazing ASL-themed quilts by Ashland, Oregon quilter Theresa Matteson Coughlan?

308

Have you ever purchased a hand-made quilt from a prison sewing program such as Fine Cell Work in London, England?

309

If you were given $50,000 with the requirement that you give it away for any quilting-related items or activities, how would you distribute the money?

310

Have you ever cried upon seeing a quilt? If so, what caused that reaction?

311

If you could magically spend an hour quilting with only one of the following, who would you choose to sew with: your great-great-grandmother or your great-great-grandson?

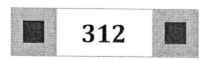

312

Merchant & Mills, in East Sussex, England, offers high-quality sewing notions, including an array of pins and needles. Do you have any of the following in your sewing basket?

☐ Bulb pins

☐ Dressmaking pins

☐ Entomology pins

☐ Glass headed pins

☐ Safety pins

☐ Toilet pins

313

Describe the most technically difficult quilt you've made.

314

Have you ever considered getting a tattoo to commemorate your quilting? If so, what would the tattoo look like, and where would you place it on your body?

315

"I only quilt on days that end in y" is a popular quilting adage. What is your favorite quilting quotation?

316

Have you ever laughed out loud upon seeing a quilt? What was so funny?

317

Have you ever stitched a quilt with healing powers? If so, who or what was healed?

318

Have you seen any of the following quilting-related plays on Broadway or in your hometown?

☐ *Blood Quilt* by Katoni Hall

☐ *Gee's Bend* by Elyzabeth Gregory Wilder

☐ *Half-Stitched, The Musical* by Martha Bolton and Wally Nason

☐ *Quilt, A Musical Celebration* by Jim Morgan, Merle Hubbard and John Schak

☐ *Quilters* by Molly Newman and Barbara Damashek

☐ *Quilting the Sun* by Grace Cavalieri

☐ *The Quiltmaker* by Catherine Bush

319

Which quilt museum is on your bucket list to visit?

☐ San Jose Museum of Quilts & Textiles, CA

☐ American Textile History Museum, MA

☐ Great Lakes Quilt Center, MSU, MI

☐ International Quilt Study Center & Museum

☐ Izumo Museum of Quilt Art, Japan

☐ Kalona Quilt & Textile Museum, IA

☐ La Conner Quilt & Textile Museum, WA

☐ Latimer Quilt and Textile Center, OR

☐ Levy County Quilt Museum, Chiefland, FL

☐ National Quilt Museum, Paducah, KY

☐ New England Quilt Museum, Lowell, MA

☐ Quilt Museum & Gallery, York, England

☐ The Quilters Hall of Fame, Marion, IN

☐ The Rocky Mountain Quilt Museum, CO

☐ Southeastern Quilt & Textile Museum, GA

☐ Texas Quilt Museum, La Grange, TX

☐ Virginia Quilt Museum, Harrisonburg, VA

☐ White Bluffs Quilt Museum, WA

☐ Wisconsin Museum of Quilts & Fiber Arts

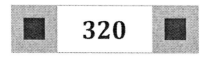

320

Do you have a quilting-related website? Have you ever visited Wayback Machine, an Internet archive service, to see snapshots of your website from years past?

321

Are you likely to be quilting in ten years? In five years?

322

Looking into your Quilting Crystal Ball, how would you describe quilts, quiltmaking and quilting communities in 2050?

What Are Your
Quilters Questions?

What Are Your
Quilters Questions?

More Books by Kyra E. Hicks

This I Accomplish:
Harriet Powers' Bible Quilt and Other Pieces

The incredible journeys of a former Georgia
slave's quilts to major American museums

More Books by Kyra E. Hicks

Martha Ann's Quilt for Queen Victoria

The true story of a young girl's fifty-year quest
to meet the queen of England . . . and present
her with a heart-felt gift.

This picture book is also available in Spanish.

How this book was made

This book was created on a PC using Microsoft Word for the text. A PDF file was produced using Adobe Acrobat Pro. The interior font is Cambria. The book cover was designed through a 99designs.com crowdsourcing contest.

Version History

1.0 November 1, 2014